Starting At Purgatory

Janice Fitzpatrick-Simmons

Salmonpoetry

Published in 1999 by
Salmon Publishing Ltd,
Cliffs of Moher, Co. Clare, Ireland
http://www.salmonpoetry.com
email: salpub@iol.ie

A catalogue record for this book is available from the British Library.

Salmon Publishing gratefully acknowledges the financial assistance of **The Arts Council/An Chomhairle Ealaíon** and the **Arts Council of Northern Ireland**.

ISBN 1 897648 65 0 Softcover

Cover design & photography by Brenda Dermody
Set by Siobhán Hutson
Printed by Techman Ireland Ltd., Dublin

For Patty Deal,
Jimmy, Ben and Anna

Acknowledgements

Acknowledgements are due to the editors of the following, in which some of these poems first appeared: Stand, Force 10, The Honest Ulsterman, Poetry Ireland, Writing Women, Janus, The Atlanta Review, Ropes.

But I have filled all of the pages planned
for this, my second, canticle, and Art
pulls at its iron bit with iron hand.

I came back from those holiest waters new,
remade, reborn, like a sun-wakened tree
that spreads new foliage to the spring dew.

The Purgatorio, Dante
translated by John Ciardi

Contents

Starting at Purgatory

Many Waters

Her Father Worries and Dreams

I said: *'It's too late, now, you've done it.'*
Yet, I meant my blessing on her unlikely marriage.

You can guess at the worry and relief for this most
unsettled daughter, with a man 21 years older.

'But he is a man Janice' – meaning her equal.
Together capable in limited ways for the long-haul;

fit for their sick child, for sex, happy according to their lights
that is to say willing to love through many nights,

happy to fight a corner, lying whole days in each others arms
wanting, wanting until the ribs expand, hair turns to feather,

how they preen with desire, how they fly in dreams.

Spring 1988

Pregnant. The fact swirls in my head
as foreign as Northern Ireland or motherhood.

I am 33 years old and hadn't realised
that I came here for this. The child is
already growing in my womb,
I watch the change in the shape of my belly –
new weight, the sore back that goes with it.
Strangely, my sweetest companion is my future
step-daughter, Anna, met at the bus
any day her father is busy. It is very rainy and cold.
We have given the child in the womb a pre-birth name,
his father has written a letter to Arbuthnot
from where he is touring now – abroad
in my home territory. I say, 'America'
out loud to the walls like an immigrant to Boston
repeating the name of remembered love.
Its name is a place like Fahan
and the strand is littered with drift.

The days pass in nest-building,
I stand on the counters in the kitchen
and wash tops of cupboards. There is
sunlight in Belfast that has never penetrated
the layers of too many Ulster Frys. I buy
scouring pads, paper lanterns, 'dirty clothes baskets,'
China birds sit above the fire in the bedroom
and I play *Graceland* and dance all by myself
in the living room of what starts
to take shape as mine, is my home too.

His ex-wife has broken-in one afternoon
drinking the whiskey I bought for Jimmy's return.

She has a dull left-wing Editor with her.
He is sitting in Jimmy's armchair, at home so to speak.
How did they get in? I unpack groceries, the baby swirls inside
and I try on calm while she lectures on the faults
of her ex-husband. Pouring them another drink
I suggest they might want to go on to Lavery's Gin Palace –
more exciting, but they'd have to pay.
They have tired me out. I sing Anna to sleep,
and watch from my bed early winter's evening
falling across back-lanes, watch light in swathes

that blocks-out the sight of many entries
and hits brick sides that glow a true fire-red.
Shadows and light almost rend the sense
of what I held was whole and solid.
The streets are quiet and I sleep
cradled in the arms of darkness, sleep
until the shake of windows wakes me. Glass bows
and strains in the sashes. The bomb leaves me breathless
in my bed. And frightens me, Ben,
knowing now this worried city, this reclaimed marsh,
your future home, the precise location of your birth.

Genetics

The sky seems to empty into the sea,
water and air mutating into each other –
all blurred horizons, no delineations, modern,
paint more important that subject –
a Séan McSweeney seascape.
And although dark is about to fall
there is no terror in it and there is no colour
but white – white horses' manes break on rock and wall,
the hard shine of winter stars are caught
in what might be a meaningless sapphire blue.

The lives of ruined lime kilns, and farms, castle towers
are mysteries wound round the heart.
I see their evidence from the window.
Their lives travel with me and with those behind me
our small distance, this brief time.
Now the life of a great-aunt
and a dear friend just dead give themselves up
to each other in an act of affection invented by myself.
Although my friend was born in 1954
she meets my aunt at the country-club where my parents
are dancing their first dance.
My mother's face is softened by first grief
because she is mourning what might have been –
a life with the first American pilot killed over France.

In a future time, in the light of an Irish winter's evening,
moon shines on my son's shoulder as he stretches, half
    discontent
toward some unknown. Say, for my sake a grandchild:
familiar, half-wild dream and dressed in white swaddling
    clothes –
star like. Starfish, Cetecea, Man, Angel, Lost Child
whatever is will be five-pointed and facing toward the sea.

The Sirens

We are in the Sirens hotel on the Liffey
and through the open window the dense,
autumn air carries Handel's *Water Music* –
'that flow endearing flow over skin, limbs...'
A candle-like light glows on the dark water
and repeats and repeats in the living body
of the river – the water is round, striated
with light. Tinfoil eyes glare gold then green.
Newly returned to the half-clean water
salmon and trout are in the flux of survival.
People are here, occasional shouts
rise from the quays.

Rivers of stars move on the fluid body
of the Liffey. The river is so dark
that the granite banks are light beside it.
These stars in the varying dome of Dublin sky
mean only light and are all light.
The night unfolds around us like a river
past the Ormond Hotel, lit with the candle's
first flicker, candles I light in memory
of each year I endured without love. There will be more,
more feasts and flesh – the silver and rose
of salmon slipping quietly like this nation
into the silken thread of my spine.

What Springs Whole From The Mind

It is summer. Marigolds and Lilies
lie deep in garden beds around the yard
and strain open, drinking change.
Heaven's surface is glass, and mirrors
the light of day that seems to spin on a string,
shaking sparks toward the ground,
these shaping and grounding the intangible,
I say these things out loud: love, duty,
family life. The grapes in the conservatory
shine, a liquid green, in a workspace that sprung
wholly made from my belief.

Once I dreamed that an angel
sang on this glass roof, stars
growing visible from behind clouds,
the warm air holding me in its arms
while music broke into familiar patterns
of words falling, as visibly as this rush of light
that ignites each bedded flower.

Dark Water

for Anna

I.

I throw stones into dark water with my step-daughter.
We aim steadily at a crevice in the rock.
Our stones bounce off each other.
We aim well and listen to the scour and clink
of sea on rock and how, when the waves draw back
there is the whistle of breath taken into a living body.
Anna wants to aim at a stone further out, a pink rock
like a scallop shell, pointed rays up in the break-water.
She winds back her arm and leg and throws
beyond my ability to throw. I am breathless
with her beauty, a power that carries, not my genes,
but something of the way I throw stones into dark water.

II.

I am in Tully on the Renvyle Peninsula
standing in the Knowlands' summer living-room.
Below me through the glass, pewter sea water,
so close that the stone floor at my feet
is its cold wash.

The ghost of Grace O'Malley is above me
in the ruined tower waiting. I search for Dolphins,
my old familiars. They ran in yesterday,
that's the season broken now –
the end of summer, blackberries and flies,
first loss.

The graveyard above O'Malley's tower
is on a knoll behind the shelf of land

that meets Atlantic waters. I walk with Tamsin
to her nephew's grave. He was born with half
a heart, taking the fourteen months
of life, holding on to it, cheating time.
I struggle with tears for my first son
who suffered and survived the surgeon's cuts,
and with the loss of my second son,
who had no shore, no sea.

The careful flowers blossom perfectly
a bag of peat moss rests by the gates.
There are many Fitzpatricks in this graveyard too.
I take in the Atlantic, try to feel Cape Cod,
their bones at rest, buried by the sea
in Bourne National Cemetery.

When Grace O'Malley sent
her son to Galway did she know
how they would hold him there?
Her bitter power shone, breaking black cloud,
the water torn by sword-like light,
silver, glowing, momentary.
When the dark closed in
Grace pointed to a small harbour,
a tower's room lit by fire, small comforts.

III.
Locked in spatial wind the Milky Way turns,
fire of stars is cold, is only the shark's cold heart,
relentless, unable to reason past hunger.

No, not just that –
in the silence of a Kerry Lough
there is the Dingle Dolphin too.

Surely, here is a spirit like our own,
passions for the other, for what is not us,
and will never be us.
We tell it to the shining stars, Orion, Cassiopeia –
record stories, write poetry, observe,
scour the town records for birth and death.
In us (if we learn to listen)
is what is here and what will be before our eyes:
water against rock, bird voices carried by wind,
three children talking by the sea, throwing stones.

In my step-daughter and son there is a power
and mystery too, no more, no less that a hurt hawk,
caught in sight of my binoculars, struggling to live.

IV.

Through several nights, all night
we loved each other again.
The tide rose, near to the new moon –
the flood waters of autumn, thinking of my parents again,
cradled in your arms, closing my eyes to walk
amid the shining Cranberry bogs of Cape Cod,
at home by the sea.

The family is gathered at this margin,
and here we take our chances,
wind back our arms, throw as we are able,
with what we have to give, call it stones,
into the dark surging Atlantic waters.

From Muck
to Muckish

The Husband's Photograph

Behind him is the farmhouse
on a shoulder of land.
Muck's tail rises darkly from bright water.
I know that rocks in reflection move and change
on the surface, chimeras, nothing solid.

And in front of the background farm
is the dog leg harbour wall...
then all that blue. That blue!

The car park is empty,
the old boathouse is empty.
A few belated boats shelter by concrete walls
set in the base of a hill.

Here, in the centre of the photograph
my husband stands, his arms spread
high and wide in blessing and friendship.

He arranges the earth for me,
kindly weather and harvest,
crazy Borage rampant, as blue as his eyes,
in clusters about his feet revealing

his comic, vulnerable and priestly nature,
ordering obedience to vision,
attempting to juggle the family from palm to palm.

Bloodroots

1

The Presidentials were disappearing
into the mist of 90°F – a week of humidity
wrapping itself into 'Dragons Breath' spiralling
to the top of the divided peak of Lafayette.
I was on Frost's badly built porch
its timber frame subsiding into the slope
of the front garden, falling into Day Lilies
and Phlox, nests of carpenter ants
in the soil about its posts.
On a tub wicker chair, a cup of coffee
on the painted wicker table next to me,
I sat watching a Ruby-Throated Hummingbird
steadily holding at the flowers and then at a sugar-feeder
hung amid the blooms, and the mist kept rising
toward thunderheads over Lafayette.

Aware of the dark windows behind me
and of his brooding presence here I waited
for the weather to decide about closing early
the little museum of Frost's years in Franconia.
Two poets worked at the back of the house,
the baby slept. This year's residents sheltered inside –
Bloodroots making their way toward winter.
The dark trees swirled in an S curve away from the lawn.
The orchard across the road had given way to heat,
something other than leaf and branch and flower.
'Ripeness is all'.

2.

Under the trees by the Wild Ammonoosuc
Jimmy and I held each other for the first time.

A wind stirred the young branches of Birch trees
by the river, Mt. Moosilauke was before us
and we stood a while here at 'Bungy Corner'.
It makes me smile to think of the company
he thought he was keeping then.
I brought him in by the kitchen door, the exact blossoms
of Bloodroot were pristine white – blood, the secret of
    their roots.
'Look,' I said and dug the bloody tubers.
From the Irish was your project
working, as you did, at the table by the door
that opened onto the porch at The Frost Place.
You seemed to burrow in, an otter nesting in a tree
close to a branch of the river where he held.

3.

My husband gave me a kiss by the river,
you remember, the Wild Amonoosuc. And then again
as we walked over the bridge that spanned the Lagan –
he waited in a terrace, close to the river, in a holt
where my sleek otter returned, ready for love,
like me a river creature.

On my wall are three of Jimmy's paintings,
all of Franconia and Panther Mountain.
'This was no playhouse but a house in earnest.'
Here are your waters, I am whole beyond confusion.

Stillbirth

Under the blue vault of a summer sky,
in the clear light of a gorgeous day,
I began to lose you. The ancient waters
were not enough, nor your father's kisses
given to me as a talisman to hold you under,
to keep you in that ebbing sea,
but the waters were all around me
and through the little window
I could see the harbour where no boats
dangled on their moorings.

Next, the bleak theatre where learning to love
and loss are one, where under the blaring lights,
woozie from drugs and the smell of blood,
I learned by heart your slender hands, your proud head.

The Granary Suite

I've been drifting in and out of sleep
this early morning, struggling with dreams
of old friends – trying to bring one to his senses,
but he cannot hear through the walls
and I am outside calling to him. I wake,
his Swan poem in my head. I feel exhausted.

Ben says; *'Mommy, Mommy, Look!'*
And I rise to this strange and perfect apartment,
poised above the river, looking out
at the bay, the Claddagh;
that is a ring of mountains round a bay.
The swift, dark vein of water flows
from the Corrib into the Claddagh.

I stand at the window, Ben says:
'Aren't they beautiful?'
Cob and pen on the river rub
their necks together in serious foreplay –
affectionate, passionate, *'Look! Wake up Dad.'*
His beak settles on the pillow of her neck,
'Aren't they beautiful, Mom?'

The male Swan mounts her.
That slender throat is now completely in his mouth.
We turn our heads away,
and are drawn back to them,
and the pulse of the river's flow.
Her tail is moving from left to right
across the surface of the water.
We have not intruded,
for he is floating a moment apart,
and she is dancing on the river.

When he swims toward her
everything is in his movements,
protective, vulnerable, stroking.
The morning sun is silver on the black water,
the mountains rising in a blue ink,
basin and bay embracing each other.
My husband settles behind us,
his arms encircling.

The Swans float together on the Corrib,
breasts touching, beaks together, heads lowered.
Their necks curve away, an S reflected in glass,
or a heart on the shimmering waters
within the ring, that is the ring of the Claddagh.

The Bell Tower

for James Merrill

Beffroi towers above Mons, a single star
too, invisible, flashing in and out like a fish
in dark lake water. Time locked
the medieval bell tower in place, a mirror
for the city – issuing warnings, ringing air,
celebrating the arrival of kings, holding tight

to a central hill, the bell ringing a tight
song, so that I walked back, time amid stars,
over a prosperous town of ancient guilds. Air
shook with the sound of bells when noise was a fish
breaking the surface of a lake. Candles in a mirror
could be seen for miles. Sound and light locked

together in the sky's density, wholly locked
in metaphor, so that bell and candle knit tight
were symbols – rippling water, candles, bright mirrors
in every window. Then the salmon of knowledge, a star
rose to the surface of the lake, a fish
that caught by the sound of bells choked on air.

They rang bells burning the girl who choked on air.
We gathered wood to burn her and rake embers of fire
        locked
into history, chased by predators, life as short as a fish.
Medieval, we begin to rise only a little, holding tight,
in Mons, everywhere. Salmon of knowledge rise, stars,
inside of us, some say vision, some say mirror

of the soul. We stayed in Hotel St. George, the gold mirror
of Beffroi above us, cobblestones underfoot, air

full of perfume – mussels and 'Lagerfelds' Sun, Moon, Stars'
Common ancestor of vertebrae – Pikaiia Chordate –
      locked
in our lives hearing bells of fear and joy held tight
to life. Water makes us. My mother called; 'You are a fish,

will you never get out of the water?' Still half fish
I answer; 'Mother, help me. You are the mirror
from which I see my animal self. Hold me tight.'
Rising from terror is slow, slow. I choke on air
of the girl burned for knowledge of flowers. Locked
in my husband's arms in Hotel St. George my nipples
      are stars

in the dark of his mouth. I am a fish in and out – a star
behind clouds, half knowing the mirror, not always
      locked
by fear and warnings, holding tight, celebrating stars, air.

Chances

My son and I walked along the strand
that was a crescent moon in the failing light.
He explained that he wanted to throw a bottle in
with a message. His sister had, a year ago,
and got a letter back from Scotland.
That is how is starts,
one voice to another over some distance –
my son drawing his arm back,
flinging his bottle in over the harbour wall.

Eurydice

1.

If I call to you from that other world,
still I am not a shade here, my thought ripples
that vast river that divides us.

And I have put on the dark clothes of
everlasting love, the kind of love you have dreamt about –
that death cannot separate. You sing of me,
I sing to the gods of another.

Pathos makes the birds swoon,
did you not see them dive before my car
in and out of the bright hedges, welcoming
and warning of all that can happen here?
The heron flew above the glass dome of the world
offering you a spiritual blessing. I have grown mandarin
under influence of many shades of blue sea or sky.

2.

When my spouse and I have appeared before now
we've been tragic, an old story that moves you, friend –
Helen and Menelaus, Tristan and Iseult,
Arthur and Guinivere. But you were so full of yourself,
correcting faults, singing to the Maenads, poor things,
our bravest knight, sleeping on the forest floor,
you said, to get closer to god.
All things are ours in friendship,
the leafiness and confusion of the world is less.

You too are a poet –
and I am married to that darkness.

Isn't that my secret, what is left unsaid
in every line; inspiring, expiring, a conspiracy
in this dark place – a place where words
and song still the chaos –
until, as is my fate, I am the movement of all words,
breath itself, the very foundation of life?

A Poet's Map of Barrington

Sun-bleached on my wall, a map in relief
of watery design, like sea in fog,
brings back every walk, a child's belief
in hearth fire, parental love, dialogue.
The sea was warm, embracing mysterious life,
when I swam in storms with my black dog
in churned brown surf –
all current and strife.
I was a Dolphin careening to shore, a rogue
not listening to rumours – weather. No grief
ever lasted. For friends and lovers I lit logs
and drift – a sign, a childlike hieroglyph.
Horse-shoe Crabs washed in on flowers and bog.
I made love on the 6th green under leaves
in the autumn sun, a watery sun-like fog
on marsh plants where garden borders weave
with sand and scutch. No proper pedagogue
led me here, labouring in ecstasy, defining flowers, seas.
More strength with every song, more ease.

Many Waters

1.

There are Yellow Flag Iris
and a broken stone head by the river-bank.
Speedwell flows from every crack,
bright blue eyes of a god
still by the water, the headwaters –
meaning maybe headstone, the clay
into which we return to a source.
The Poplars murmur overhead
and as I walk, the sound of waters
flowing, that if it's not exactly voices
reminds me of the sea murmuring on still days
(the Poplars and the sea don't make a human sound
but the river does).

Once on another continent I jumped
naked into an icy pool of the River Gale.
The darkness of the river swallowed my body.
I loved its absolute cold,
the feel of granite in its touch.
Trillium grew on the banks of the river in profusion,
finding the cool earth of river habitable –
Trillium's pristine flowers a deepest, blood red
or snow-white – the earth and water's heart
(you mustn't pick them).

Later and further down the river
I bought five acres
and swam under a stone shelf by an old river-mill
under the little waterfall, learning the Gale,
its moods as it poured over me,
its blessing of simple physical pleasure,
and endurance to cold.

2.

I grew in a sheltered bay
of the western Atlantic, the sea around me
my amniotic waters, a source of life,
salty, caressing, dangerous. From her waters
I pulled wonders; fish that could fly, sharks
that sent my father into a panic,
a panic that rises now in my throat
with my own children.

All my best dreams happen by the Irish Sea,
my home – Portmuck's dark and white rock falling
steeply to the water and the shoulder of a harbour.
Last night Charlie, our dog, leapt to greet
my husband in his boat returning.

A small cast of loved ones were around me
travellers on the journey. My children,
Ben and Anna, waded out to meet him.
Under a pale grey sky, we pulled his boat to shore.
A grey-blue Bottle Nose Dolphin jumped in the harbour
     water.
An Oyster Catcher settled easily
on Anna's outstretched hand.
Curlews flew in formation, tight
against the harbour's rock wall.

3.

When in my dream I wake from my dream
by the Yellow Iris and Forget-Me-Not,
at the river's edge
I am walking and thinking about my mother
and our love,
a seed blown amid Poplars

settling by the river's edge.
And then my mother's watery presence:
'At death it would be good to be immersed
again in river water.'
Yes, maybe –
into the Gale that flows
its stormy way over mountains
into other rivers, into the sea.

From Muck to Muckish

Fossil rock from the Sligo coast, Spanish bowls,
shells and sea-glass from Greencastle's hidden strand,
the mirrored earrings that light this face that dreams
beside you, are waiting to be packed and we begin
to close the door on our first home together.

The road west is growing shorter, a day trip includes
an autumn drive around Hornhead. Rainbows
are electric and hung over rock-cliff and Atlantic
to be taken as a blessing on our future here.
The storm-dark is cut by light, Sheephaven's waters
glowing, glass-like, unbroken by great winds
blowing in from the west. The grass and bracken
are russet, amber and burnt-gold, and move,
a woman's burnished hair glimpsed in the dark mirror
of this road that is one-way; is a loop that takes you to
    the edge
and back to the nape of a headland that holds,
in its coil of road, a part of our future that we gaze
back at now, paused in the car, trying to imagine
our life here, the way we've taken. Inscrutable Muckish
appears from clouds and mist, and disappears.

Loss is also memory – the Black-Backed Gull voices
around the hollow of my chest, Curlews flying
in tight formation around the sea-stack of my neck,
the Linnets in hedges lifting their wings
about my ears in dizzy flight.
Closing the door on little sorrows,
we make our way together to business appointments
and architects – old life and new world meeting
in the still centre of the storm
and what we drive toward willingly now.

Sophie's Cottage

Solid light comes from the Cabbage-Rose dish,
pink and green, that I have found here
covered in black grime and now rescued.
That dish is my symbol of the beginnings of home,
of the love and pain it takes to make a space
that will speak to what we know.
The 'Laughing Cavalier' jug
is back on the window sill where I found it –
his arms are crossed,
one leg over the other, his ecstatic face set there.

Muckish is trying to send me a poem,
for these lives passed without speech,
trying to sort this telegram.
The wires are tapping,
the silence is broken by the language of birds,
by a Cuckoo hammering at joy. The wild, high clouds
pour in from the Atlantic with a wind I can hear
and wrap silver plumes around the mountain height.

Sophie, I set you as a seal on my heart,
as a seal on my arm, writing this poem
with your dish washed clean in front of me.
The flowers in the garden are taking the changing light,
the glow on them and your faint presence
haunt the cottage door
of what will grow into us and up from
the deep roots of our lives.

Dawlish

The river tamed by canal locks
runs through the centre of town
and the black swans float under
Christmas lights that hang in perpetual
celebration. Two black Swans together,
and two cygnets floating on the dark river
of late autumn heat and light
cause a faint shimmer of deeper darkness
moving across the water.

I feel our trace in the Swans' shimmer,
the mystery of complication,
our dark reflection in the water.
Your other family's gathered not far from here
for a wedding; and us four, our family
are in happy retreat from the party,
drawn to locks and Swans to watch for a sign
that didn't come until dinner in the guise
of a joking, handsome Indian waiter.
He flicked his lighter at the candle, he flicked again,
then gracefully took the lighter we offered.
He smiled a buddha smile
and great food followed, Pilau,
Tandoori Prawns, Chicken Korma, Rogan Josh,
the pleasures in our own contentment.

The canal where the black Swans are floating
divides the river from the sea,
it marks one passage and leads toward another.
Tomorrow before we make our journey home
we will watch the Swans who seem to me an emblem
of past sorrow, we will watch them feed and glide,
the river taking them where they need to go.

Your Own Story

You were the woman in the white satin
gold embroidered gown
spinning yourself in front of the mirror.
You chose that cruise and wore the dress
to the Captain's table and drank gin
in the stateroom with your husband,
whose anger choked the goodness in him.
But you sat there alone, the dusk falling about you,
your husband at the casino on board,
and you said to yourself *'one day at a time –'*
the words an addict uses,
to conquer the want inside.
And how could you love? Love was short-lived
like the lives of the children buried inside of you,
the memory of holding your babies in your arms,
cradling their brief lives.
'Honor and Cherish' were words
you said in a ceremony when you were young.
We say love and then say,
'but what does it mean?'
Tenderness, banished from the heart by pain.
What we do to our words makes the angels cry.
The smoke from your cigarette
filled the cabin and the sun fell in a red flame,
the shoulder of a Caribbean island
swirled in a tropical haze of distant greens,
the darkening turquoise water seeming to envelope
you, where I've left you, in your own story,
in a room gone blank.

Ballroom Dancing

I want you to look back
over the grey and purple sunrise
of a day in that other Donegal,
say on holiday with Tony and Bill,
camping near Greencastle's ruins,
walking to the Smugglers' Inn in the rain,
pissed, flirting with actresses, full of yourselves,
serious – a premonition of where
you've found yourself
in the lap of family under Muckish.

I want you to be always
kissing Eileen by the Foyle
in the wanton dark.
Stars pulse out the rhyme
of love and you are young
and singing sometimes in the Corinthian,
dancing there – ballroom dances
that I have learned like Latin verbs
to please my father.

'Here is the delicate turn,
the side step of the waltz,'
my father said. 'Turn your head,
come into the rhythm
and movement by looking back
over your shoulder.'

And I look back,
into the tentative eyes of a thirty year old,
a woman coming into herself,
bending over the water of the Gale.
One of your selves, the stranger,

scoops water in his hands
for his mistress, Mars and Venus
rise that evening low on the horizon,
dazzling those two caught there in time.

'And here is the trick,' my father said;
'To keep in step with your partner
dip and sweep a little forward
while you look back.'

Pillow Talk

Behind this smile is battledress
and a warp-spasm for this fag-end of a century.
The bully-boys, in the circularity of time,
are all wearing skirts and make-up
and well-made jackets to flatter their straight bodies.
And they have a line of talk, that if you deny
is at best unhealthy, and at worst treason.
They walk through committees, down corridors of power.
It was always thus, and no better now than ever.
We are one race.

A few of us are heroes in our own way,
young Finns or Cuchulainns
fighting out the bit for the love of idea,
or for the love of place, for a beloved who holds
the idea of things on the palm of a disengendered hand,
trembling with the beauty of it all, with desire,
with the flow of rivers like the Owencarrow
that ran red with the blood of Saints
arguing over a work of art and the terror it contains.

If there is a battle-glow on me love,
it is from frustration and despair,
for my spear is pointed at what future?
I am sick with the politics of my own sex,
I am sick with the gossip and jokes of the other.
We are one race. I cradle my son's head
in the crook of my arm,
I love him and you, and that is enough.
When I walk on the strand
I do not fight the waves.
I try to teach myself the hero's art of patience
and articulation.

A Famine Poem

I hold onto the idea of love, its past and present
that washes us with the regularity of tides.
I do not like the fact that you had other wives.
I do not like your stories of your youth here –
Olivia-Ann Wilde, her body in Wild Chamomile
and Sea-Oats where we hold on today

in this sand and scutch shelter,
the beat of the Atlantic on rocky inlets,
estuary waters. You cradle
my hair and back and ease me free.

Beloved, ambiguous, certain beloved,
you who make me feel at home and alien,
today the rain mists the higher ground
and I am a Choctaw walking lightly as I am able
over the hungry grass.

The Feast

There is something in the Blackberry brambles
making noise, feasting on the juice
of rancid berries. I bathe
in the autumn light on a green
plastic chair.

The Fuchsia flowers
have made the pathway red
and the branches bosky, tipped with light,
alive. The sky is very clear
and there is a sharpness about things;
the crooked stalks bent by westerlies,
the electric green grass, the grey donkey
sweating and braying in the field.

Charlie, our sleeping dog, is shining
black in the sun. Ben shouts
'*Rain*' from the front garden, a shower
of sword play. '*Have at thee,*' he shouts.
A Heron rises from behind the trees
gliding on ancient wings.

Fugitive in the Geriatric Wing

The sons and daughters – 18 of them –
are like Finches round winter beds.
The movements of winter birds in beds
are nervous, and her children; 18 of them,
flit from room to dayroom whispering
what they are able, and holding hands.
The birds' low sounds hover under
the last Rose leaves. Magpies come and go,
bright and dark wings a shadow above the bed.

The curtains and wallpaper cheer
this 50s wing of Letterkenny Hospital.
The curtains hang badly and the wallpaper
is dilapidated. There are pink Lilies
and Rosebuds too, pink with blue-green foliage
on a background like a hazy morning.
The first of the bright sun razors
late mist.

The wallpaper suggests your mother's
favourite chair, covered in sail cloth, the smell
of her sitting there where she called to you:
'Come.'

The gift of flowers the children
gave are wilting in the vase –
once such bright colours
on the ward's long sill.
All night *Medical 2* fills
with the sound of letting go –
white and yellow Shasta Daisies, red Carnations,
Forget-me-nots.

Surfaces

After days of rain the dark-leaved
Sycamores glisten, dark candles in the new sun.
The stone walls, leaves of Hollyhocks,
Love-in-a-Mist shine, as if the light
glowing came from inside their dark interiors,
a transmutation of the fire at the core
of water and earth, the light within
rushing toward its blue spinning surface.

Middle Age

It's the way the fall air holds the water
about the mountains as if you were looking
at its deep blue, its purple and grey,
its bosky substance through sheerest gauze,
so that what we say here is 'It's a soft day'.

and what informs the heart then is
a dream-like seeing, a longing
for autumn bright days to last, a melancholia
that belongs to the season
of ripeness.

And from this ripeness of Blackberries,
past the 'Tears of God' fallen on the roadside
you come with your arms outstretched
under the bruising light.

Sulphur

Maybe,
no-one has told you about
the falling away of friends,
and the way the soul feels,
as if it has fallen into water
that is dark and reflective,
full of weeds that,
if you try to swim, would catch
your ankles and drown you
in the muddy depths.

Old friends are trying
to live their lives without the memory of you
and they have no time
to fool around; their marriages, careers
and self esteem are on the line.
You are part of their bad past,
they don't deny it. You ring
for a talk, for a token word
and you sense their power,
in the dis-engagement, although
a love dirge just appeared
for you or for your lost child
in a New York journal.

I thank you for your perfect American
concern, and I assure you we are all just fine.
Of course, the most crazy
of us all, Allen Ginsberg, finally
found how to live well. Ten years
in NYC as a stockbroker helped
him find a modicum of peace
and demand certain cloths

and waters and hotels when he read,
Oh Naomi!

But in Belfast when he sang:
'Don't smoke, don't smoke
the American dope, dope
dope for 20 minutes
(and I don't smoke),
it made me want to.

You have lost your way
old friend, in the ways of power.
But I remember you without
a price, vulnerable in the
cold rain that snows about us.

Whatever bargains you made
with the devil, don't tell me.

Starting at Purgatory

Whitehead To Dublin

1.
I glimpse seals on rocks from the carriage window,
the train rounds the bend and they are gone,
their appearance so brief I wonder if I really saw them.

The morning is a chill misted autumn one
and I have been left to the train by husband and child
to make my way on a rare solitary visit
back to the city I left for Belfast. The bad thing
about Central Station is the switch you have to make
from one platform to another, running up one steep
    corridor
and down another to catch the Dublin train.

The train makes me restless, not sad but nostalgic.
How I came to him; my little case
crammed with books and high heels.
There is a river that flows between neat,
high banks – Oxbows over flat countryside.
From the train I make out a sign that says
The Ulster Way, beside the water the trail is wet
and green with reeds that grow on the banks.
I watch an old man and the light that falls
with such radiance on him as he faces into the sun.
He raises his hand smiling and turns to walk away.
The river flows so slow that algae's viridian body can't
    break up
– it quivers and undulates in the melting sun.

My first few trips on this train
going the other way, from Dublin to Belfast
were fraught with uncertainty, alive with the future.

Still the gold fields of Barley rolled in the distance.
That night we knew life was lifting in me
we walked by a river that opens to a small still lake.
On the left bank a house with curved windows shone
    in darkness.
Our tentative hands reached toward each other in the
    blinding mist;
and high above us and clear the drifting Milky Way,
its thousand million stars.

Hospital Visits

2.

With my lover, who is as stiff-hearted as me,
I made my way round the little hill that leads
to The Royal Victoria Hospital for Sick Children.
We touched him through glass, touched what we
    could of him.
When the Doctor said that the infant would need
more surgery we re-evaluated our estimate of perfect
    health,
held him close when the nurse followed us. We held
and ached around the base of him, around the mystic
    mountain.
I dreamed of snowy heights, an instant of clarity
on the long road. You drove us to Errigal
and every Donegal headland to restore me.
I could only think of the cliffs and water,
the danger of the rocks below.

After months in hospital Ben's first words early:
'What's that?' 'A flower,' I said.
It was spring, Snowdrops, Daffodils and all the pristine
flowers were making their stiff way toward the sun.

To have a sick child is to bring care, and to have him
    survive is joy.
We plant the gifts of friends, Roses and Hydrangeas
Hollyhocks and Delphiniums.

The harbour below us was dogged by teenagers
driving cars relentlessly round the public lot at midnight.
Restless anyway with this second pregnancy, I am awake.
To lose a child late in pregnancy is to age.

Loss, loss and never happier.

I sat out on a folding chair by the Night-Scented Stock,
near the Roses in the front garden,
viewing the sunset over Jura and the moonrise
over the Isle of Man at midnight.
I thought if we were able to see before us
we would run from the pain and difficulty.
And I was glad that we only know our circling by doing
     the dance.
Orion's Belt was just visible with its three dancing stars.

Northeast to Northwest

3.
There are problems you can fight
and problems that you cannot fight.
It is difficult to fight bigotry and impossible
to fight power except by laying down your life.
So, like many before us
we resigned our land to powers and debtors
and headed for the hills. We had a friend,
brought skills with us, and here we are at home.

Ben is a magical age, the same as Cuchulainn
when he killed the hound. He is learning to fiddle,
to write well, to speak Irish,
and hold on to what he has.
His step-sister holds the key to his heart and she is kind.
I bless that girl and the woman she will be.
They love it here.

At first to wrench their hearts from home
was anger and tears, but the move taught all of us,
and me again, to open to the changing fates –
the weather of time. It was a cold first winter
in the rented house. Snow covered Muckish until April,
lambs perished in the unexpected cold.
Three graduate students in spare bedrooms
three nights a week. Exhausted.

But our students did their work,
handing poems in, obsessed as we –
painting five rooms of the new place without complaint.
And the ferry to Tory their final day of term,
all of us too broke to stay – taking the return boat home

through afternoon into twilight. Errigal and Muckish
were a dark crown floating on the water. The rising dark
did not close the evening sky that first night of summer,
the tang of salt in the air, Venus visible,
the first of the summer stars.

Afterword

4.

In my dream I flew with an angel,
the earth rushed past beneath us,
the muscles in my back and neck
tingled with the weight of wings.
But that was a dream, and if an angel
came to me then his message was physical –
the joy of the body imagining flight.

No ghosts of poets haunt me,
but their living words reach through time,
are borne to me on the white wings
of the page and its conundrums.
My fingers move with possibility
covering the distance of unmeasured space.

Where The Roads Lead

for Mary Reid

1. At Beltony

The sun of early November bears down
on the stone circle causing the mist to rise
from the sodden ground of a year
with no summer and early gales.
At Beltony, set on a small green hill between green hills,
my sight is aimed through the bare branches
to Barnesmore Gap and the sea.

Behind me there are hills too,
covered with leaveless trees
of Columbcille's foretelling –
evergreens block the sight line from here
to Grianan of Aileach. Shadows fall
and steam rises from the half-buried
male and female marking stones,
and from the finger stone
that marks the journey's way.

I walk the descending path
through the darkness of pines
and the brief wet glitter of twigs and moss.

2. St. Patrick's Purgatory

The ferryman steering St. Bridgid is old and dark.
Yeats's giant bird of the lake is in a dreaming underwater
November hibernation communing with generations
who have made their way up this riven valley
to the lough and sulphurous island's Basilica,
at one with knights and poets,
shopkeepers and maids, traditions echo.

Derg water slaps and foams
about the solid boat, and the sun is aching
and bright on a Heron's wing as it rises
from a dark rock in the lake.
To step on the receiving dock in the emptiness of winter
is to hear only the soundings of belief
and half-belief through the old chapel,
round and round the stones of the station,
in the tired wind clanging the penitents' bell –
Mea culpa, Mea culpa, Mea culpa.

Blame me too for my physical nature
for what I liked the most was the wide window
in the new hostel where I could look out across
the water and fields and watch the procession
of myself projected there –
that dream-like country of the past
unreeling, making its way toward me
in blazing autumn light, travelling the path
that led to this valley, this lake, this island.